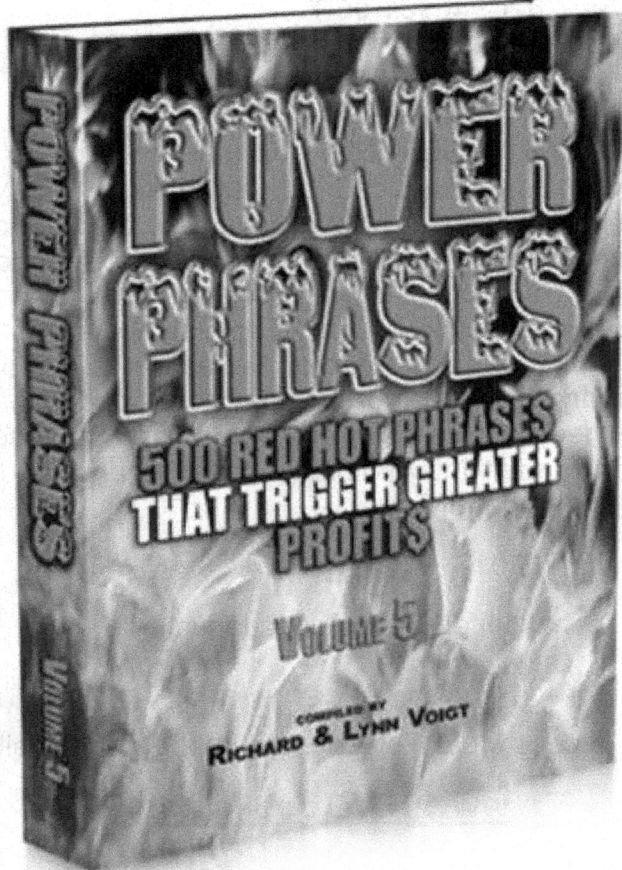

POWER PHRASES – Vol. 5
500 Power Phrases That Trigger Greater Profits

ISBN-13: 978-1-940961-05-7
ISBN-10: 194096105X

First Printing, 2013

Printed in the United States of America

To Access More Powerful Marketing Tools Visit:

www.RIVObooks.com

www.RIVOinc.com

www.WisconsinGarden.com

POWER PHRASES

Volume 5

500 POWER PHRASES THAT TRIGGER GREATER PROFITS

-·|·-•·*")""*·•._-·|-_•**•-·|·-•·*")"")*·•-·|·-
·|·-•·.*.   .·._-·|-_•.   .·._-·|·-•·*. .·._-·|·-

Compiled by
Richard & Lynn Voigt
I.M. Education Specialists

Introduction:

Powerful Phrases, Headlines, Sub Headlines, Slogans, Bullet Points and Interview Sound Bites are perhaps the most powerful marketing tools mankind has ever created. They are the lifeblood behind every business venture are the ultimate secret weapon of Millionaire Marketers.

No matter whether you are introducing or promoting a brand new product, teaching a "How To" skill, building a website, or simply sending an email, using the perfect power phrase is crucial to capturing and holding eyeballs and producing greater marketing profits.

In today's world every word you use has measurable impact. Each word can produce emotional psychological buttons that trigger psychological reactions. Successful advertisers understand that using an effective power phrase is a true art form that turns "wants" into instant gratification "needs." Once artfully triggered, any niche market can instantly create more protifable conversions.

Now it's your turn to personalize this incredible collection of 500 Power Phrases in ways that instantly advance your own effective marketing skills as you create new and power phrases, slogans, presentations, bullet points, or interview sound bites that take you to the next level.

Whether starting or running a small business, writing an ad, coming up with a memorable slogan, making a major corporate presentation, bullet points, creating a video, writing a book, searching for the perfect slogan, teaching a lesson or book report, your creative use of these Power Phrases can capture more eyeballs and produce some amazing rewards quickly turning you into a Marketing Genius. Now, it's your turn to make the magic happen!

POWER PHRASES

Volume 5 – 2001 - 2500

500 Power Phrases That Trigger Greater Profits

Begin Selecting & Customizing Your Perfect Marketing Phrase

2001	When Silence Is Golden
2002	$1000 In Coupon Savings
2003	No Techno Babble Here
2004	Refocus Setbacks
2005	Watch Your Lame Competition Become Envious
2006	Playing With Your Joy Stick Just Got Better
2007	Launch Your Own Grass Roots Campaign
2008	We Can Help Who You Are
2009	It Will Disappear Soon
2010	How Are These Problems Secretly Driving Your Life
2011	CAVEAT What Works And What To Avoid
2012	The Best Of The Best
2013	Essential Sparkplug For Marketing Ignition
2014	A Startling Epiphany
2015	Why People Have Problems With This Step
2016	Writing An Effective Press Release
2017	Asset Deficient Website Draining Your Future
2018	Know Where You're Going
2019	Lying On The Beach Soaking Up The Rays
2020	Simply Saying WOW Is The New Normal
2021	The Single Piece That Made The Entire Puzzle Make Sense

2022	**Furious Price Hikes**
2023	**The Big Dream Killer - EXCUSES**
2024	**Make Your Point Bold And Clear**
2025	**Don't Let People Guess What To Do**
2026	**If You Can Do This Process**
2027	**The Exact Blueprint To Follow**
2028	**Pierced By 301 Nails And Retains Full Air Pressure**
2029	**Bring On Your Biggest Result**
2030	**Turn To The Future Now**
2031	**This Is All Part Of The Journey**
2032	**Pass This On**
2033	**I Just Found This Niche**
2034	**Social Networking Expands Your Empire**
2035	**What Works The Best**
2036	**How To Win With A Strategy**
2037	**What - No Agenda**
2038	**Would You Rather Be Rich Or Wealthy**
2039	**Be Your Own Niche King Of The Hill**
2040	**Always Provide Real Time Stats**
2041	**If You Do Kindle Consider This**
2042	**Earn Online Income**
2043	**A Glimpse Into Tomorrow**
2044	**When Length Of Domain Registration Matters**
2045	**Your Ads Are Your Lifeline To True Success Online**
2046	**The Value Chain Is Broken**
2047	**Stretch Your Lists Beyond Limitation**
2048	**Unlimited Source Energy**
2049	**No Over Scripted Here**
2050	**Earn A Track Record**
2051	**Squashing Sunday Sadness**
2052	**I Wish I Could Give You A Hug**
2053	**No Sponsoring Needed**
2054	**What Pay Per Click Advertising Is And How It Works**
2055	**Delivery Failure Notifications Limiting Your Profits**
2056	**A Lead Generating System Focused On Converting Sales**
2057	**It's All About Possibilities**
2058	**Fall In Love All Over Again**
2059	**Give People A Reason**

2060	With The Right System It's Very Easy
2061	Click For Credits
2062	Lost Money I Didn't Even Know About
2063	Jump Start Your Creativity
2064	What Happened Immediately
2065	We Warned You To Join Us
2066	My Hand In Friendship
2067	Service And Patriotism
2068	Nothing To Lose
2069	It's Like A Personal Assistant
2070	This Is A Must-Watch
2071	Grow It Into An Empire
2072	This Expense Is No Longer Required
2073	The Niche Always Starts With A Need
2074	Prominent Bullets
2075	Organic Search Results
2076	First In And Last To Leave
2077	Logic Justifies Emotion Emotion Drives Sales
2078	Jumping Dangerous Hoops
2079	All Of Us Have These Common Problems
2080	Reset Your Industry
2081	Would A Conversion Rate Of 70% Be Of Interest
2082	What's Inside Your Business
2083	Build A Sticky Blog
2084	What's Your Digital Weakness
2085	Brimming With Incredible Information
2086	Cut Your Risks To Zero
2087	On Time And Below Budget
2088	More Than Casual Contemplation
2089	It's A Good Idea To Register
2090	Work That Is More Fulfilling
2091	Next Stop Nowhere
2092	Think Less Accomplish More
2093	Learning To Walk Before You Run
2094	These People Know The Truth
2095	Reap The Rewards From My Efforts
2096	Learn How To Sell Your Product
2097	Watch Your Niche

2098	Time Management Tips
2099	Now That's What We Call Turnkey
2100	Promoting Growth And Expansion
2101	Make A Fortune With Cutting Edge Technology
2102	My Girl Friend Hates This
2103	Add This Site To Your Favorites
2104	Doing All The Right Things
2105	We Just Can't Help It
2106	Are They Shutting Down Your IPO Again
2107	Read What Real People Think
2108	Consumers Will Beg You To Take Their Money
2109	It's A Crime
2110	Call Me Crazy But This Insane Offer Is Absolutely Free
2111	Maybe You're Worrying Too Much
2112	Jobless And Directionless
2113	Make Eye Contact
2114	I'm Ready To Give You The Push You Need
2115	One Simple Strategy
2116	Claim Hidden Keys That Open Doors
2117	The Ease Factor
2118	The Freedom To Work In Your PJs
2119	Ramp Up Your Online Business
2120	Your VIP Application Form
2121	Surprise And Engage Your Audience
2122	Two Versions Of The Truth
2123	For Your Self Esteem
2124	The Big Question Still Left Unanswered
2125	Instant Buzz For Your Site
2126	Test Website Colors
2127	Fighting So Hard To Sell
2128	How To Start Success
2129	Thanks For Sharing This With Your List
2130	Get The Deal In Writing
2131	Dramatically Accelerate Hot Product Sales
2132	Attract Exact Targeted Audiences
2133	Most Brilliant Group Of Minds Ever Imagined
2134	Create Your Mission Statement
2135	You've Just Finished Saving For Your Kids' College Fund

2136	Is Your Site A Serious Contender
2137	The Key To Separating Yourself From The Crowd
2138	Suck vs. Awesome
2139	Free Social Media Marketing
2140	Get Your Special Discount Now
2141	Efficient Disciplined And Systemized
2142	Are You Willing To Try Something New
2143	An Unfolding Plan
2144	What Do You Hate The Most
2145	Hitting The Knee Of The Curve
2146	A Marketing Riddle
2147	Ever Ask - How Do You Start A Business
2148	Winter Into Wisconsin
2149	If You Have More Time Than Money
2150	Overcoming These Major Obstacles
2151	Profit From Radio Advertising With These 7 Keys
2152	Getting Your New Free Website Up And Running
2153	Create A Plan Then Make It Happen
2154	Makes A Great Gift
2155	It's The Coffee Stupid
2156	Targeted And Affordable
2157	Blog And Ping Master Course
2158	Be Polite And Respectful To Everyone
2159	Marketing Drips And Drops
2160	This Is A Tall Order
2161	Constantly Break And Pause
2162	Interview Style Video
2163	Turning To Us For Expert Guidance
2164	Loyal And Faithful
2165	One Step Ahead
2166	Getting Them To Commit To The Next Step
2167	Avoiding Desperate Situations
2168	Where Will You Be 5 Years From Now
2169	Valley Wash Out
2170	The Rarest Form Of Action
2171	Nice And Easy
2172	You Must Satisfy Their Curiosity
2173	People Want To Save Money

2174	You Could Use This To Run Your Own Giveaway
2175	Even For Humble Beginning Online Entrepreneurs
2176	Super Discount Limited
2177	This Free Stuff Can Help
2178	Editable Prefilled Terms And Conditions And Privacy Pages
2179	Would This Catch Your Attention
2180	Creating A Larger Purpose
2181	All Season Long
2182	Faith Family Friends Fun And Financial Freedom
2183	Principles Of Change
2184	Is The Corruption Over
2185	As Long As It Needs To Be
2186	I Want To Show You The Real Process
2187	Being Bold Increases Response
2188	Tell Us What You're Thinking
2189	Baring All Doesn't Mean Getting Naked
2190	Baby Boomers On Fire
2191	There's No Way The Reader Can Lose Focus
2192	What Are You Looking To Leave Behind
2193	Inefficiently Priced Market
2194	Vital-Profits For Free Ads
2195	Why People Want To Be Sold
2196	Seven Dollar Solution
2197	What's The Ideal Goal That You Would Like To Achieve
2198	A Round Of Applause
2199	Making Money Blogging For Dollars
2200	Even Distributors Are Feeling The Pinch
2201	Choose The Approach Best For You
2202	Systems Have More Perceived Value
2203	The Art Of Solving Problems
2204	Purging My Way To Freedom From Email Clutter
2205	From A Successful Vantage Point
2206	Healthy Niches That Make Money
2207	The Best vs. The Rest
2208	Being Here Today Is Perfect Timing
2209	On Top Of Everything
2210	Lead The Way
2211	Showing A Softer Side

2212	Special Introductory Trial
2213	Make Decisions On How To Live Your Life
2214	Is Pinnacle Leadership Dying
2215	SEO Ranking Recipes
2216	What Comes To Mind
2217	Won't Nearly Cost You As Much
2218	It's No Longer Enough
2219	A Little-Known Tactic
2220	Join This New Gold Rush Opportunity Today
2221	Uploading Files To Your Server
2222	Plan For Growth
2223	How To Use Twitter To Crank Up Your Promo Power
2224	Free This Weekend
2225	Breathe Sleep And Dream Of Marketing
2226	You Can Stop Typing
2227	Large Scale Mastermining
2228	Easy Uploads To Your PC
2229	Guaranteed To Work
2230	The Best Kept Secret In
2231	How Many Times Have You Asked Yourself
2232	Upgrade Your Necktop Computer
2233	Everything Is Just Fine
2234	Testing Your Secret Cross Sells
2235	Any Affiliate Programs You Want
2236	Instant Opt-in Profits
2237	These Strategies Are Different
2238	Time To Turn People On
2239	Everyone Has A Unique Story To Tell
2240	Your Website Has Been Suspended
2241	I Expect This Offer To Go Very Quickly
2242	Wandering Aimlessly
2243	Value Added Service
2244	Marketing Face Value
2245	How Most People Screw Up Their Headlines
2246	Bridge The Gap To Wealth
2247	It Just Can't Get Any Easier
2248	We've Hired The Best Developers
2249	Friday Fortune Frontiers

2250	Send $.75 To Help Cover Postage And Handling
2251	Easiest Way To Get Your Products Online
2252	Want To Create A Software Empire
2253	When Can You Start
2254	Are They Saying No Deal To Your Ads
2255	What Happens When You Focus On Just Bad Stuff
2256	Don't Miss Monday
2257	Attacking The Marketing Day
2258	So Let's Get Started
2259	Why Develop A Friendly Long Term Relationship
2260	Time's Running Out
2261	Your Choice Continue To Struggle Or Shine
2262	Taste Your New Business
2263	Open Your Ears And Fill In The Blanks
2264	Don't Be Seduced By Distractions
2265	I've Personally Tested It
2266	Don't Outsource Your Marketing And Sales
2267	Click Here To Get My List
2268	Simply Learn More Here
2269	Hit Every 3-Point Shot
2270	You Can Use My Entire Staff
2271	Knowing How To Help Them Get Through Their Own Fears
2272	A Very Special Holiday Gift
2273	Motivated To Take Action
2274	Those Guys Suck
2275	Want To Get In Your Own Business
2276	Modular Concepts Called Knowledge
2277	Be More Beautiful
2278	This Is One Of The Few
2279	Funny Freakday Friday
2280	Does This Make You Look Strange
2281	Over The Next Few Days You'll Receive
2282	Lacking A Solid Commitment
2283	Powerfully Renewing
2284	Guaranteed For 100 Years
2285	A Decade Of Growth
2286	It's A Great eBook
2287	Loopholes That End Up Ripping You Off

2288	Bombed And Down
2289	Technical Developments That Can Hinder Success
2290	Transferable Private Label Rights
2291	This Is How It All Weaves Together
2292	Sorry It Just Sold Out
2293	Give Each Section Their Own Headline
2294	Sling This Into Your Wallet
2295	Completely Sold Out In Minutes
2296	Today's Dream - Tomorrow's Reality
2297	Find Yourself First
2298	So What's The Real Secret
2299	Pecking Order Superstitions
2300	A Full Expression Of Who You Are
2301	Eliminate Hassles And Tribulations
2302	Let Machines Sell Your Products
2303	May Commission Payment
2304	Thinking Of You
2305	Why Watch Streaming Video Free
2306	Rethink Your Current Situation
2307	I Find Myself Reviewing The Material Over And Over
2308	Fine Tune Your Elevator Pitch
2309	We've Perfected A System
2310	Is This A Myth Or Secret
2311	Why Employment Sucks
2312	Let's Take A Quick Break
2313	Hardcore Copywriter
2314	What's Relevant To Your Business
2315	Earn Income 24 Hours A Day 7 Days A Week
2316	Someone Is Fibbing
2317	10 Boundless Ways To Anchor Down More Sales
2318	Optimized For Color
2319	This Is Very Different
2320	Lead The Best Team
2321	Talk To 10 People In Your Related Niche
2322	Building A Test Bed Tool
2323	Are You The Cultural Warrior
2324	Everything Matters
2325	How To Put Up A Website

2326	Is Your Opt-In List A Joke
2327	Achieve An Appropriate Boost
2328	It's Bonus Time
2329	The Unrefined Multi-Tasking Wasteland
2330	Non-Functional Decoration
2331	When You Can't Find A Cure
2332	Get A Fresh Idea Every Day
2333	Tip The Scale For Your Prospects
2334	Change In Perception
2335	This Will Start To Change Things
2336	There Are Only 24 Hours In Today
2337	Making Money On Internet
2338	Make It Jump Off The Page
2339	Huge Discount For The First 100 Buyers
2340	This Is A Pack Of My Best
2341	Is Your Pot Of Gold Empty
2342	Tasks Well Suited
2343	A Real Business Guide For Entrepreneurs
2344	Don't Summarize What You Just Said
2345	More Bills Because You're Earning More Money
2346	Start Small
2347	I've Been Where You've Been
2348	People You Sponsor
2349	No Longer Tethered
2350	How To Dig Your Way Out
2351	By The Bucket Full
2352	Why They Stopped Justifying Mistakes
2353	Why Just Pick The Low Hanging Fruit
2354	Listen To The Video Script
2355	Show They You've Been There
2356	Being On Camera Is A Skill
2357	Before The Internet Existed
2358	Enjoy The Satisfaction It Produces
2359	I'm Not Talking About That
2360	Dramatically Boost Your Sales
2361	Don't Put This Off Till Tomorrow
2362	Triumph Over Adversity
2363	Traffic Is The Marketing Lifeblood

15

2364	An Irresistible Idea You Can't Ignore
2365	Begin Ruling Your Mind
2366	Web Army Knife
2367	I Really Hope This Helps
2368	Just Coasting To Retirement
2369	This Can Easily Blow Up In Your Face
2370	Consider Your Reaction When You Land On A Squeeze Page
2371	Fast Fantastic And Free
2372	Can You Spell N-O B-R-A-I-N-E-R
2373	How To Set Up Your Own Membership Site
2374	Say No If You Must But You'll Regret It
2375	Truly Simple Solutions For Complex Problems
2376	Design It Yourself
2377	Some Call This The Google Bounce
2378	New Search Navigation
2379	Timing Is Everything Act Now And Grab Your Free Bonus
2380	Creating Your Own Reality
2381	Imagine There's No Food In Your Marketing House
2382	Busy Days Are Here Again
2383	These Results Were Astounding
2384	Steal This Ebook
2385	Super Design Tricks
2386	A Day That Can Really Change Your Life
2387	Why Isn't This Taught In Kindergarten
2388	Your Only Goal Is Creating Useful Valuable Information
2389	Want To Strike It Rich In The Internet Gold Rush
2390	Free $500 Victoria Secret CPA Offer
2391	Failure By Trial And Error
2392	Idea Solution For People Out Of Work
2393	Thanks Guys And We'll See You Soon
2394	Maximize Your Income
2395	Your Affiliate Tool Box
2396	I Finally Found A Real Advertising Offer That Works
2397	Training On How To Succeed Online
2398	We Have Great Deals On Most Everything
2399	Hidden Legacy
2400	Does Product Creation Scare You To Death
2401	Are Your Secondary Headlines Equally Powerful

2402	**Creativity Ingenuity And Entrepreneurship Will Fail Without This**
2403	**Instantly Become More Productive**
2404	**Ready To Finally Take Action**
2405	**The Force Behind The Headlines**
2406	**What Doesn't Get Done**
2407	**What Is Its Motivation**
2408	**Let's Tackle The Issue Of Time**
2409	**SEO Collateral Damage**
2410	**Fun Ideas Flooding The Mind**
2411	**Consumption Matters**
2412	**This Pet Needs A Second Chance**
2413	**Huge Research Surprise**
2414	**Tactics For Niche Broadcasting**
2415	**Your Patience Is About To Be Massively Rewarded**
2416	**Scarcity Drives Customers**
2417	**A Whole Lot Of Fun In The Machine**
2418	**Walk On Water For Your Prospects**
2419	**Products You Want**
2420	**Cheat Sheet For Generating Leads**
2421	**What Is That Thing You've Learned To Solve Their Need**
2422	**Turning Profits Into Real Money**
2423	**No Fluff No Filler No Fine Print No BS**
2424	**Say Your Name**
2425	**The Early Click Gets The Order**
2426	**Free Line Content**
2427	**What Were You Expecting - Fluff**
2428	**Earn More Tomorrow**
2429	**A Word Of Warning**
2430	**In A Nutshell**
2431	**Turns Clicks Into Commitment**
2432	**Here's An Idea**
2433	**Copywriting And Editing**
2434	**Programs Products And Services Started By Listening To Needs**
2435	**Focus On The Most Powerful 20%**
2436	**Tend To Lose Track Of Time**
2437	**I Don't Want To Work Like A Dog - Do You**
2438	**100% Profit Margin**
2439	**That Would Be Really Great**

17

2440	Like Some Tools To Help
2441	Take Responsibility For Mistakes And Move Forward
2442	We're Even Going To Sweeten The Deal
2443	Avoid Bait And Switch Methods
2444	Turn Your Marketing Frown Upside Down
2445	Know Who The Enemy Is
2446	Customized To Meet Your Needs
2447	What's Your Reality Habit
2448	Don't Give Away Future Royalties
2449	Add More Personality And Resonance
2450	It's Not In The History Books Yet
2451	You've Asked For It
2452	Mind Map Mining
2453	I Cannot Say Enough
2454	It's About Time
2455	Is It Bonus Time Already
2456	It's Something We Have To Practice And Do Ourselves
2457	Extra Income Online
2458	There's Nothing Wrong With Money
2459	Brilliant Simplicity At Work
2460	You Won't Let This Slip Away
2461	Unedited Testimonials
2462	Barely Inhabit Your Body
2463	Send Your Words Upwards And Outwards
2464	When You Demand Extraordinary Service
2465	How They Earned Cash Without Technical Skills
2466	Deadly Infiltration Tears Down Conversion Resistance
2467	Fuel Your Passion
2468	People Spend More On Their Car Than Their Brain
2469	How Do You Find Lasting Happiness
2470	Show Me The Features
2471	F. Y. E. O.
2472	A Very Active Safelist - Join Now
2473	WOW Guess What Happened
2474	Would You Know If You Saw It
2475	Avoid Fashion Fad Clothing
2476	This Can All Be Yours
2477	Stunning Success Without Frustration

18

2478	Still Working For Peanuts
2479	They Order More Than They Can Sell
2480	Reveal Details About Yourself
2481	Miss It Or Miss Out
2482	Open Our Marketing And PR Folders
2483	Statute Of Limitation
2484	Let Me Squeeze Your Page
2485	Count Your Umm And Aaahs
2486	How To Get Floods Of Free Traffic
2487	Jump Start Ideas
2488	This Is Where Everything Is Heading
2489	3 Myths Of Successful Marketing Online
2490	Exclusive Never-Before-Released Set Of Videos
2491	Compensated Only On Results
2492	More Than Just A Slight Edge
2493	Get Better To Grow Larger
2494	Achieved Millionaire Status
2495	Ever Tried Singing For Your Supper
2496	Moving A Blog To Your Own URL
2497	You Gotta See This
2498	This Is A Massive Market
2499	Guru Doubler
2500	How To Survive Any Storm In The Economy

Lynn and I hope that this "Think Tank" volume series of 500 Hot Phrases will helped you clearly paint your dreams, sell your ideas, and market your messages, propelling each of your ideas and projects toward incredible success. Watch for our next Volume!

We truly wish you the very best and look forward to hearing your success stories.

Concluding Thoughts:

Ever success is built upon a preparing a strong foundation, having a clear vision, and taking positive action each and every day. If you've been searching for a new lifestyle, then you'll find this book directive and inspirational. You can open it to any page and let that page help you rethink possibilities, consider new ideas, open new opportunities, and ultimately experience a more successful and fulfilling lifestyle.

Every problem has a solution! Regardless of your current situation or circumstance, know that you have the power and responsibility to redirect your life in any direction you choose. Simply start thinking about and research the kind of lifestyle that truly appeals to your heart. Begin your new journey by learning everything you can about your chosen subject. When you make that commitment, you'll open more unexpected doors to unique opportunities than imagined.

"Creative Thought Is The Only Reality
Everything Else Is Merely The By-Product Of That Thought."
- Walter Russell

So why not start thinking **BIGGER? It won't cost you any more.** It all starts by never allowing your current life's situation, environment, or so-called friends to limit your path to a happier, healthier, and successful life. After all, whose life is this?

Make a decision to focus on learning something new each and every day. Begin attracting your ideal lifestyle by doing something you love and enjoy. As difficult as it may be, don't allow money to limit your dreams. Focus on the kind of thoughts that make you feel good. Once you learn how to control your focus, you'll have a great chance to see your dreams take shape. You've finally learn to harness the power you always had within, a Universal Energy stream that flows 365/24/7 in any direction your project your thoughts, Good or Bad. Want proof? The thoughts you currently believe and project reflect the life you're currently living. Therefore, if your life isn't happening, change your thoughts, and change your life. It's something only you can hold, visualize, and project, living your dream come true.

Find yourself a mentor and spend more time with people who truly appreciate, support, and foster your dreams. Life may be short, but the thoughts we hold can make our life wider and more fulfilling.

About The Authors:

Richard and Lynn develop creative strategies that paint dreams, sell ideas, & market messages   Together, they present a unique team-approach, working side-by-side, helping clients pursue their passions while sharing their skills and diverse expertise as authors, artists, inventors, entrepreneurs, & Internet marketing education specialists.

Teaching by example, they mentor proven self-publishing services, graphic design, video production, domain acquisition, and marketing research of behalf of their company, RIVO Inc – RIVO Marketing, since 1997. They've created & produced hundreds of videos, self-published dozens of books on a wide variety of topics and created thousands of original works of fine art, while refining their Internet Marketing techniques, mentoring programs, and related business website development.

Their mission is to continually uncover new products and services, test new strategies, and network useful solutions with off and online entrepreneurs, small business owners, writers, local artists, models, teachers, students, and marketing professionals.

Their goal is to help clients create an action plan that discovers and connects the missing pieces of the success puzzle. The goals they foster create multiple streams of income for today's volatile economic climate. Their motto is: "Do the work once and allow the work to create additional streams of income for a lifetime."

Feel free to contact them if you have questions or would like to tap into their talents and expertise. They appreciate your feedback and look forward to hearing your success stories.

Contact:
Richard & Lynn Voigt - RIVO
I. M. Education Specialists

RIVO INC - RIVO Marketing
13720 West Keefe Avenue
Brookfield, Wisconsin 53005 – USA
Email: support@RIVOinc.com
Website: www.RIVObooks.com
Website: www.WisconsinGarden.com

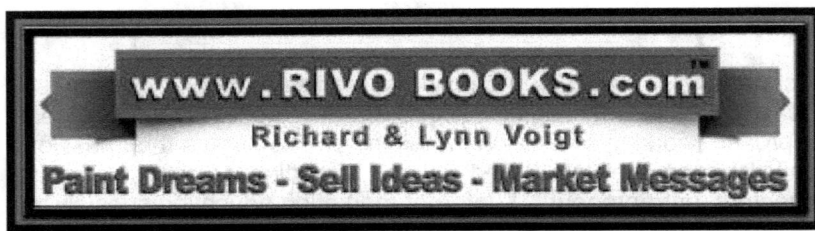

Visit Lynn's Garden: www.WisconsinGarden.com
view hundreds of great garden video blogs Tips

See Richard's Unique Artwork: www.RIVOart.com
view over 3,000 original Fine-Art compositions

Our Book Titles Now Available On Amazon:

THE GOLDEN VAULT OF MOTIVATIONAL QUOTATIONS
Words of Wisdom from The Greatest Minds & Leaders

BABY NAME .ME - 21,400 Names & Nicknames
For Family, Friends, Pets, Natural & Man-Objects

DOODLE DESIGNS Volumes 1-3
For Professionals & Kids Of All Ages
DOODLE DESIGNS – Vol. 1
DOODLE DESIGNS – Vol. 2
DOODLE DESIGNS Coloring Book Vol. 3

Work MORE Accomplish LESS Get FIRED!

ACTION HEADLINES That Drive Emotions – Volumes 1- 6
Paint Dreams, Sell Ideas & Market Your Message
Action Headlines That Drive Emotions Vol. 1
Action Headlines That Drive Emotions Vol. 2
Action Headlines That Drive Emotions Vol. 3
Action Headlines That Drive Emotions Vol. 4
Action Headlines That Drive Emotions Vol. 5
Action Headlines That Drive Emotions Vol. 6

IDIOMS – IDIOMS - IDIOMS
6,450 Popular Expressions That Put Words In Your Mouth

The CLICHÉ BIBLE - 8,400 Clichés For Sports Fanatics
& Lovers Of Popular Expressions

MORE THAN WORDS
5000+ Marketing Phrases That Sell

HYPNOTIC PHRASING
WARNING-This Book Teaches You How To Grab Eyeballs

YOUR RIGHT TO WEALTH
Becoming Wealthy Isn't Hard When You Know How

WI GARDEN – Let's Get Dirty
Our Wisconsin Garden Guide Promoting Delicious, Healthier Home-Grown Fresh Food, With Tools, Tips, & Ideas That Inspire Gardeners!

MONETIZE YOUR SOCIAL LIFE
Earn Extra Income While Having Fun Online

BABY NAMES
21,400 Unique Baby Names & Nicknames

FUNNY HEADLINES vol. 1
3,500 Outrageous Silly Brain Toots

FUNNY HEADLINES vol. 2
3,500 Outrageous Silly Brain Toots

JOBS
10,240 Career Paths That Can Change Your Life!

MONEY WORDS
Powerful Phrases That Million Dollar Copywriters Use To Make Piles Of Cash On Demand!

GARDEN QUOTATIONS
400 Garden Quotes From The Earth To Your Soul

HEADLINE STARTERS
175,000 Words That Paint Dreams, Sell Ideas, And Market Your Message

BABY NAMES
25,350 Baby Names & Nicknames For Your Family Friends & Pets
  697 pages 7,000 Names with Origin & Meaning plus Top 100 Names, And 2,000 Most Popular Names

CURIOUS WORDS
15,800 Words That Expand Your Mind And Change Your Life

INSPIRING THOUGHTS
That Inspire Happiness, Success & A Clearer Understanding Of Life

MARKETING EYEBALLS
100 Ideas That Can Add Unlimited Subscribers To Your Lists

SECOND OF FIVE
My Early Years- From Birth To High School

POWER PHRASES – Individual Volumes 1 - 10
500 Power Phrases That Trigger Greater Profits

POWER PHRASES Pro Edition – Volumes 1-10 (Complete Series)
5000 Power Phrases That Trigger Greater Profits

POWER PHRASES Pro Edition Volumes 1-10 (Complete Series)
5000 Power Phrases That Trigger Greater Profits

What do Marketing Millionaires know that you don't? They know how to pull money out of thin air by using their secret language of Power Phrases.

This Pro Edition of 5000 Red Hot Power Phrases not only saves you time and money but will help jump-start your creative brain in ways you may have never considered. Simply open this amazing collection to any page and find your perfect power phrase. All it may take is simply adding or replacing ONE word. It's simple, quick, and easy!

1. **Want to create more powerful profitable campaign offers?**
2. **Thinking of revitalizing a more professional business identity?**
3. **Want to update old product or service media advertisements?**
4. **Searching for fresh ideas that could improve sales and profits?**
5. **Looking for brand new ways to create stronger media sales copy?**
6. **Ready to use millionaire strategies advancing you to the next level?**

5000 POWER PHRASES is exclusively for professional Internet Marketers, authors,advertisers, executives, business owners, TV & radio reporters, entrepreneurs, administrators, managers, supervisors, teachers and students who want to find and access unique phrases for marketing slogans, presentation bullet points, and interview sound bites that powerfully paint dreams, sell ideas, and market your message.

Stop wasting valuable time, money, and energy racking your brain for new ideas. Create more profitable power phrase marketing campaigns for all your products, services, slogans, bullet points, and interview sound bites that finally grab and hold people's attention and trigger greater profits?

You now have a very powerful and professional marketing tool in your hand. We are confident that you know how to use it wisely in order to maximize the potential of all your marketing campaigns! Lynn and I **Thank You** for your support and purchase.

CLAIM 500 MORE POWER PHRASES!

Thank you for purchasing this eBook and in doing so we would like to send you **500 More Red Hot Power Phrases for FREE!**

When you post a **positive review of this Book on Amazon Books** under this title you'll receive an additional **500 POWER PHRASES.** Your review may also be sent directly to us.

Your request must be received within 30-days of purchase. Once your positive Book review is posted and verified, simply email the following to **(500@RIVOinc.com)**:

1. Full Name of Purchaser
2. Email address
3. Paypal Invoice Number
4. Copy of your posted Book Review*

Once we receive the above, we'll send you 500 Power Phrases **(PDF)** emailed to the address you provided.

Visit: www.RIVObooks.com for additional volumes as they become available including the Pro Edition of 5000 Red Hot Power Phrases that say what you mean to say and trigger greater profits.

Lynn and I look forward to your written comments and suggestions as we love hearing from each of our readers.

Richard & Lynn Voigt
RIVO Inc – RIVO Marketing
13720 West Keefe Avenue
Brookfield, Wisconsin 53005 USA
Telephone: (262) 783-5335
www.RIVObooks.com

P. S. If you love gardening, catch us on www.WisconsinGarden.com

*NOTE: This offer is valid providing it does not violate the terms of service of the entity with whom you made this purchase. Duplicate or incomplete entries will also not be eligible and this offer is limited to one request per email address. All eligible review submissions become the property of RIVO Inc - RIVO Marketing – RIVO books and may be used as promotional testimonials ads on RIVO Inc websites. This offer may be withdrawn at any time without prior written notice.

www.ingramcontent.com/pod-product-compliance
Lightning Source LLC
Chambersburg PA
CBHW060709280326
41933CB00012B/2364